Inside Her a River of Snow was Traveling

Poems

Also by Toni Thomas:

Chosen
Fast as Lightening
Walking on Water
Blue Halo
Ace Raider of the Unfathomable Universe
You'll be Fast as Lightning Coveting my Painted Tail
Hotsy Totsy Ballroom
Love Adrift in the City of Stars
In the Pink Arms of the City
In the Kingdom of Longing
The Things We Don't Know
In the Boarding House for Unclaimed Girls
They Became Wing Perfect and Flew
Unburdened Kisses
Bandits Come and Remove Her Body in the Night
There is This
Here
The Smooth White Vanishing
Perishing in the Rain
A Different Measure of Moonlight
In Her Soul the Pale Rooms of the Moon were Wandering
The Secret Language of River

Inside Her a River of Snow was Traveling

Poems

First published in 2024 by Annalese Press
134 Towngate
Netherthong
Holmfirth
West Yorkshire HD9 3XZ
England

Copyright © 2013 Toni Thomas
Published 2024

All characters and situations appearing in these pages are creatures of the imagination and in the service of poetry.
Any resemblance to real persons living or dead, is purely coincidental.

All rights reserved. No part of this publication may be reproduced, stored, or transmitted in any form, or by any means electronic, mechanical or photocopying, recording or otherwise, without the express written permission of the publisher.

Cover design and layout by Peter Wadsworth
Portrait of a Young Woman, Edgar Degas, 1885

British Library Cataloguing-in-Publication Data
A catalogue record for this book is available on request from the British Library.

ISBN 978-1-7394457-9-9

Contents

Part One   *The Bruised and Battered that Sometimes Passes for Lovemaking*

They can't be kissing again	3
We weren't busted yet	4
It was queer hearing that sing song	6
It was a stirabout	8
My sister and I are visiting	9
He kept threatening her	12
I wasn't talking dirty about him	14

Part Two   *Yucky Midnight*

Were you like this	19
I want to say	20
When we began to eat yucky midnight	22
It's four days into January	24
When I can't take it anymore	26
You pussy the moon	27

Part Three   *An Epistle of Shot Gunned Birds*

I am biding my time	31
It was the Hallelujah Chorus	32
Mavis says we're going for a lady's night out	34
I am thinking about surrender	36
I want to forgive	37
My papa is a hard man	39

Part Four   *The Perilous Nature of Landscapes*

My sister has gained weight	43
I used to Christmas carol	44
I was learning to spell	46
The lights are glowing	48
It was the school play	51
It has been a bad day for forecasts	53
Over in Wattsville they're getting ready	56
I'm not going anywhere fast	58

Part Five   *Paradise on a Pole Stick*

Am I a coward that counters the wind   63
See you later   65
It's a creepy crawly inchworm in the snow   67
For how many hours, days, years   69

Part Six   *The Language the Trees Preach*

You won't believe it   73
Was I made for love   74
My name is Dorothy   75
It's the summer of my life coming   77

Epilogue   *Finch Feeding*

Sometimes when we hear
the memoir of a life   81

I believe in kindness. Also in mischief.
Also in singing, especially when singing is not
necessarily prescribed.

Mary Oliver

I said to the almond tree
'sister speak to me of God.'
And the almond tree blossomed.

Nikos Kazantzakis

Part One

The Bruised and Battered that Sometimes Passes for Lovemaking

They can't be kissing again

there in the hallway
bird pecking their love

we'd grown sick of it
the soupy looks, soppy handrails
twin fish and chips
they bought afterwards at the store
later on the unexpected transom
of tears towing
the way their hands kept dividing
then marrying.

They can't be up to it again
there in the big bed
noisy as shotguns
my brother dragging me
into the yard without a coat
the chickens noisy
everything white
the busted stroller, three wheeler
thresher
pickup with its mangled frame

my brother promising me
when I grow big enough
he'll teach me how to hunt coyotes
break the neck of a chicken
about the bruised and battered
that sometimes passes for lovemaking.

We weren't busted yet

it wasn't the mud season
I hadn't learned how to dissect mice
stir in a floozy skirt
invite boys.
Snow everywhere, tired gutted roads
the pond frozen
my mother cooking up
potato casseroles, stew.

We weren't busted yet
made to sit straight in school rooms
memorize numbers
the clocks hadn't borrowed us
the corner store was still loaded
with hard candy
five varieties of bubblegum
sat on the shelf.

We laid down on the grass
fanned our arms into snow angels
while plows barreled through town
salted the roads
my father recited Bruins wins
wax winged our blades.

We weren't busted yet
never noticed the gray sky

lumps in our mattress
never heard the woman up the road
cry over her foreclosed house
noticed the way Emily lugs
rocks in her shoulder bag
eats from the snow.

It was queer hearing that sing song

as if they'd made up
green wreathed their past
the one with bars, rock and roll
card playing

found mercy
would set table
emerge like nightingales
into some Sunday best
that was for a short while
enough for them.

It was queer marking time
sueting our lunch bread
lathing the hell out of it
forcing my sister to
gulp down her milk
never admit famine.

Back then I was merciless
whiplashed her pigtails
water pistoled
till later on
calm was never a mark of her.

We harmonized with stray birds
hand-me-downs
a blue trampoline
tried to turn the other cheek
turn the other cheek
as if God was watching

as if we were going somewhere
those folks on disability weren't freezing
in the trailer park down the road.

I vouched to be a livery stable for my sister
nail the strict in her
never let star-struck kisses, fake compliments
find a home.

It was queer hearing them sing song
patched up as a swim tube with no more leak.
Afterwards, mama would go out, arrive back
with donuts, two dozen of them.
I'd eat the glaze off four or five
till my daddy would sock my head
say for sure *you better start finishing what you start*!

It was a stirabout

kind of a hodgepodge
she made on Sundays
torn bread, milk, sugar
currents, cinnamon

my brother, the glory and hog
gobbling so hard
he'd land half on his lap
my mother tireless
always tableclothing her love.

It was a stirabout
lumpy and prone to scald
if the oven was set high

a throw together kind of thing.
No one could figure out the recipe
not even Aunt Jewel
could drag it out of my mother's mouth.

My sister and I are visiting

the aunt's house.
She lives in Texas. Hot weather
air conditioning and all.
My mama says we get to wear
cowboy boots with spurs
that my sister can pigtail her hair
under a tall Stetson
ride a horse if my aunt's willing.

It's part of their grand plan for us.
Two weeks of souped up romance
for my daddy and her.
Have the house to themselves from
morning to midnight.
My mama won't even let the Christmas lights
on the front porch get boxed
says we need some sparkle around here
and I know she means something more
than twinkle bulbs.
They have been married fifteen years
and then some.
Old as far as my sister and I are concerned.
Past the age of drive-in movies
back seat cooing in pickups.

My sister claims he barely
notices mama anymore
stays out late night drinking
that even when she bakes

her tangiest meatloaf
he takes one bite, complains
tells her *stick to the recipe.*

She was once a ballroom dancer
before my daddy stepped in.
Used to work in a law office in Prineville
says she wore slinky dresses
went dancing on the weekends
made good pay, bought a new Nissan
but he put a stop to it.
Told her no soon to be the mother of his kids
was going to go sashaying around
indenture herself like a slave.
He was raised churchgoing.

My mama and daddy are having
a honeymoon of sorts.
My sister says she's bought two
new nightgowns, been drinking
TrimQuick shakes at breakfast and lunch
to cut down on the calories
is bench pressing in Mable C's basement.

He will be happy about it.
Can't help but notice the way he
talks up strangers.
Eyes my sister's teenage friends
says my mom doesn't look good

because she don't take care of herself right
pay the bills promptly
buy the right cuts of meat
insist on a raise at the school.

He's a stickler when it comes to
managing things
likes the food placed dead center on his plate
his eggs over easy, onion in the harsh browns.
I've seen him walk away from a breakfast table
when there's no hot sauce
call it *a load of horseshit*
turn my mama's face from joyous to fallen.

We are going to Texas.
Leave by bus tomorrow.
The house is being sponged clean
and my mama's been polishing her voice
skin lotioning her legs.
Says when we get back there'll be
a baked ham meal waiting
and we say *Yes, mama*
but secretly aren't counting our chickens
before they hatch.

He kept threatening her

My father kept losing his way home.
Nobody said anything.
The pork chops grown cold at the table.
My sister and I silent as plant pots
bent over the hall desk
me working my multiplication
my sister crayoning ladybugs
sure that someday they'd carry us.

One afternoon my mama stopped believing
in words, the inflated nature of them
stopped frying up his pork chops
peeling the dust off our sofa
sunnysiding his eggs

slumped in her morning chair
refused to get up
unlearned words, grew sullen
as if speech had become road kill.

It was February.
nearly all the birds flown south
the seed in our yard feeder
sopping wet, moldy.

It can take months for a thaw
to come over things
unmangle the path
sent shoots of thin crocus

a stammer of purple
up through the earth.

We learned to be extra good that year
didn't chip paint, trouble the coat racks
ask for what wasn't coming.
Learned to eat packaged buns
easy bake pizza, corned beef hash
grow the lean arm of our hearts
into faultless trees praying.

I wasn't talking dirty about him

Promise Mama.
It was not me
I never use words like that.

My sister is about to have her
mouth scrubbed for her four
letter words.

We don't put up with that in our house
not with my grandpa coming soon
and my sister pissed cause she's been
ousted out of her room and into the basement.
My grandpa can't do stairs.

I'm not sure I like her pouty lips
the way my grandpa`s speech slurs
he munches tobacco
till his teeth turn brown.

My mama says we got no choice
somebody has to take him in
it's the decent thing to do
since he has no wife
a shit load of prescriptions.

You can see by his silence
the way he walks out of rooms

blasts his cassette player in the garage
that my daddy's not pleased.

I glue my mouth shut.
Have learned good that there are times
nothing you can do about something
that some people sing before they
can walk
others need the death scared out of them
before they ever going to learn to
carry a tune.

My daddy is in the last of these categories.
He ain't about to lighten his heart
till a thunderbolt come ramming
and maybe my mama gets control
of her weight
learns again to sweet talk
the dark out of him.

My grandpa is coming.
My mama's only living relative.
She and her brother raised by him
the hard measure of his hand.
She tells me one year there was
no Christmas, not even a tree
as if the birth of God was
delayed in the field

Mary with no manger
and her ornery dad coming too close
till she took the piping hot iron
raised it off the board
pressed it to his hand like hell stinging.

Says she paid a big price.
No Christmas. No presents that year.
Her brother hiding himself away
in the yard shed.
Her papa grown absent
at some other woman's trailer park
the one with the war vets
half-starved dogs.

I wasn't talking dirty to nobody.
Promise.
But my mama doesn't believe her
keeps telling us to chasten our hearts
let God lead
as if hot irons don't amount to anything
just mirrors of some past life
old scabs
no bleeding.

Part Two

Yucky Midnight

Were you like this

when I married you
did the birds perk up
watch from the bushes
pause over the downy nest of our lips?

Did you already feel owing
bugged with women, your job
the leather whips you say
the world keeps flashing?

That day you brought me daisies
a fist of them new from your yard.
It was the start of April.
I was twenty two, cute in my cutoffs
midriff top
the yard pulsing
with newfound crocus
the daisies stuffed in a milk jug
already practicing summer.

My hands held compost, coffee grind
wanted to make good, coax double big
out of the rose bushes I'd been digging
into my daddy's side yard.

Too much damn shade
where I planted them.
But that day you weren't saying.

I want to say

don't make me ride a dead horse
til I'm sick with April
see something more than the squalor of me.
You hairpin words
chop wood
stack it neat as shop meat.

I am almost forty
not sure what I'll do when the kids leave
still vacuum up piles of dog hair
gift wrap meals
work the school cafeteria
scooping fake cheese
onto the children's plates?

My friend Melanie isn't ever going
to be left behind.
She lifts weights, denies french fries
meets the bullshit of her man with
store bought cheesecake
a chiseled waist.

Henry isn't sure he wants to
go over to the mill or be a plumber
talks about animal science at the state university
getting out of here
not that we've got much saved.

You will be busting mad
already I'm hearing

that damn boy gonna waste his life
at the rate he's going!
I'm always trying to keep peace
hear both sides
pamper with pecans.

Treena's growing so fast
her jean legs don't keep up
gets to be *papa's favorite*
and I confess to thudding
in my boots when I see the measure
of attention you offer up to her.
She's cute and you know it
always buying her new tops
Van sneakers.

Can we bribe love
pay it down in plush sweaters
coo words that don't leak
is there a contamination in being
almost invincible?
Why do you barely look at me
as if I am the cat with one eye
faulty fixture pinned to the wall?

When we began to eat yucky midnight

with a tarnished spoon
memorize the past as broken plates
derailed kisses
I half wanted to poison your meals
watch death make a more
decent human out of you.

Crush my heart for saying all this
I'm ashamed, thinking less than
the best of my man
but you deal in blue scissors
swallow the dark
map the grass with guardrails.

My words never manage to keep up
with your debate team
the way you toothpick meals
pit bull my eyelet
keep those brunettes baited
complain about the way I wash shirts
stack a dishwasher
tell me you've been busting ass
and what have I got to show for my day.

As if I'm some scattered, uneven woman
a turn the key kind of dim witted plastic toy
that squawks on command
later offers up a lap dance

cries herself stupid over things.
Irrational, irresponsible you label me
in front of the kids, warn them to
think right, not like your mama

as if I have scotch broom growing in my head
only half-baked meatballs
can't stir the tapioca
read a political column
as if only you, big papa, do things right
can whip up the wind
daddy long leg the dark
make everyone love you speechless.

It's four days into January

and we're looking at a weekend of snow.
You run the town plow on Saturdays
like to keep busy, watch football, ice hockey
nurse beer, rush our daughter to the mall
buy her new boots, froufrou scarves, a fancy phone.
Like the idea of being a pal with the kids
making sure neither of them need me.
Tell me lies about where you've been
those late night private emails.

When I confide in you about my fears
over other women, Treena's friends
too many sleepovers, the thick mascara
taking over her sweet fourteen year old face
you laugh, tell our daughter
your mom's complaining about the makeup again.
I know it's crazy but I feel totally undermined
and my daughter ends up not speaking to me
claims *you don't understand me like dad.*

I'm worried about our son's sullen
the way his mood snaps, can reel out a torrent
of abuse–
*you're past useless mama. Never did amount
to anything. What have you accomplished for yourself*
while you sit grinning
as if my whole life is judged and juried

by the cruel eye of your needs.
Is our son becoming a spitting image of someone?

I'm trying to figure out when it all went wrong
when I started to bruise, coil in on myself
stop feeling free to step out with friends
find a few laughs
started to forget that little girl rattling
and the other nameless one
that sultry woman
who curses and stirs up such a storm in me.

When I can't take it anymore

the mean remarks
backstage women
endless instruction on *the right way*
to plant strawberries
load a dishwasher
vagrant the dark
manage our small as a prick sex life

then that pussycat steps in
the one who vandalizes panties, hot lips
tempts, holds back
comes in a flood

is a tease
beckoning paradise.

You pussy the moon

shove on a CD of love songs
calculate merlot, wine glasses
dim light.

My leather boots stay zipped.
I raise up on tip toe
rub your thighs
want to travel your blue river
slow birth
flash naked beneath eyelet
draw you close
forget the distances.

Want to believe that no one
ever kicks midnight
chooses to use the moon
as a punch bag.

Part Three

An Epistle of Shot Gunned Birds

I am biding my time

crazy as it is
two kids crammed in snow boots
you always sure you know
how to get the better of things.
My patience grown of God's least
handsome, strident sycamore.

I am biding my time
trying to knot hope
into the most flirty of friends
tuck away my slinky skirts
curling iron
fake leopard muff.

Am I a coast train waiting
to happen
red siren
map of some lost navigation
disguised honk toy?

Every day the world casts down
hailstorms
straight lines kids
wants to make me an
epistle of tarmacked roads
shot gunned birds.

It was the Hallelujah Chorus

that used to get me.
I can't explain it
what singing can do
how it lifts cold days
plants ranunculus.

You kept your mouth shut
listened with your head's laundry.
Didn't sing.

It was the Hallelujah Chorus
that used to get me.
Not because the voices were great
arrived at every note
but because their spirits were willing
and the pastor's sermons
rang with April.
I've had enough of the other kind
to last a lifetime.

My daughter and son stopped coming
claim they are too old for that stuff
we've put God in a cage
strangled the life out of him.
But I know in a crisis
there's at least one tender being
that'll be there for them.

Am I a parody of my once self
the leper who sees in the rain
wants to come clean

always wants to come clean
but somehow my life keeps slipping?

Stall an old dog long enough and
sure as hell he'll learn new tricks
you say that to me
as if it answers things
as if we are stalled trucks
in need of a mend job.

I keep hearing the praise come.
Arrive in secret envelopes.
My day lilies holding tight till
they ride past winter
into their showy silks.

Mavis says we're going for a lady's night out

and I'm tickled
not sure if she's doing it cause
she feels sorry for me
or there's nobody else willing
but we're making our way Saturday night
and I have no idea what I'm going to wear.

My black dress doesn't fit right
thanks to the fuller mercy of my hips
that dress is ten years old but
I refuse to give up on it
and if the snow report is true
we may be driving in five inches of new stuff
which probably means I'll be stuck
in black lug boots over my boxy coat
not the sexiest thing in the world
but hell, at this stage of my life
who's probably going to look anyway.

She says C.J.'s in Wattsville is going to have
a live band at the weekend and even if
I'm not sure I remember how to dance
we can sway our bodies as if Nashville is calling.

I'm going for a lady's night out this weekend.
Mavis says you can *piss pants* if you give me
any shit about it
that I should stop feeling I need to keep you
from lonely.

I'm guessing my kids will be pissed
miffed I'm inconveniencing them, not their taxi
there to make them fish fry, get pop at the store.
Treena will eye me up and down before I leave
complain about the way my clothes don't match
my sweater shows bulge.
Henry will interrogate *what time you getting back*
who you seeing, how I'm planning to waste the night
and you, I'm guessing you're going to sulk
till the sky goes black
make some snide offhand remark
about floozy women out to pick up young guys
hurt the hell out of me
resent the fact that for a while I have the nerve
to be taking a break from this.

I am thinking about surrender

the misunderstood parts
how some folks can't figure out
the way I put up with things
never divorce the old man
keep his words from piercing.

Sometimes I get pulverized by his blades.
The ones that thorn his heart
make him sure nobody in the world
is going to stick it to him.

I make bread, stew
let them linger in his blue mouth
like a stopgap against pain
corn field my words that in his ear
turn into sharp glass, barbed edges.

Nobody knows the endurance
that travels me
the hand-me-downs, thankless meals
how hard it is to turn the other cheek
when snowballs keep coming

the way I avalanche my past
into a woman's ice sculpture so rock hard
it can suck up the cold.

I want to forgive

the trespasses in my life
know the fractured hearts
that tried to stride here
how broken down, pummeled
our lives can get

that for all his dogged
and good intentions
my husband keeps feeling smacked by the wind
and I know I can't save him

my children shimmying into go-carts
skimpy skirts, trying to fit in
be the Rolls Royce everybody wants
as if love grows on a candy striped awning
can sidestep the rain.

I want to forgive
but my thoughts aren't always willing
dial up catastrophe
badly dealt hands

that's why God keeps inking my door
with bits of springtime
reminders I'm not a failed person
wimp
there's no shame in turning
the other cheek.

At the community church
everybody greets me

mostly older folks, a few families
the slow voiced minister.
The chairs aren't rock hard
you can set your cares in them.
Even though I don't arrive each week
or leak anything much about the
pains that are needling me
everybody knows my name.

I come out feeling surrendered
damp moped
able to keep my man half in love
my children in lunchmeat
the tired wheels of my heart turning

able to eat up the snow.

My papa is a hard man

to please.
Never imagined years later
I'd be taking him in
trying to make a smooth final bed.
That man swore his socks off
never heard the meadow lark
of my voice calling

never worshipped the satin
of our mama's ways
his eyes so knee deep in boy hurt
even the birds deserted him.

I'm trying to imagine losing his mama
to pneumonia, his alcoholic dad
years in an orphanage
being sexually abused
a new high school twice a year.
I just can't get my mind around these things.
Don't know what to do or say.

My papa still yells at me like I am a defeated toy
girl who just can't get stuff right
whether it's marrying the right man
missing the 2nd turn left to his dentist
cooking the pot roast moist as his bread pudding

doesn't find much pleasure in me
the way I navigate the world
attempt to dam up the scald of heat waves

make a decent meal
not go perishing.

Almost every man I have ever loved
has been the prospect of a sudden
bruise coming.
I hate to admit that.
The cruelty that can encumber things.
How God leans on such a
fragile stem.

Part Four

The Perilous Nature of Landscapes

My sister has gained weight

too many french fries, bags of chips
tells me nobody in her fifth grade class
has a kind word for her.

My mama's sing song has turned
into the thump of fry pans
cry fits, low calorie dressing.
She powder puff things invisible
then late night eats two bowls of ice cream

tells me I'm hard on my sister
that I stare too much, sulk
make people nervous
says *you're fifteen, grown up already*
should know better than this.

I used to Christmas carol

up at the Green Hills Community Church
where they'd herd us into boy and girl sections
tell us to wear warm coats, look presentable.

I knew all the songs.
oh come all thee faithful, silent night, holy night
hark the herald angels sing...glory to the new born king
knew that Daniel B was being forced to sing with us
and Harriot H was bribed by her mother
who has a penchant for serious churchgoing
too many crosses.

It was the year my voice started to crack.
Mama kept trying to disguise the fact
wanted me to stay boyish forever
be her *sweet son.*

We traveled to shut in houses, the trailer park
apartment buildings in a grey van.
The seats smelt of spent leather, dead Twinkies
Pastor Bob's cigars
reminded me of men who travel poker rooms
gamble their wealth.

I was sixteen.
Wasn't yet trying to decide between
the paper mill, the state college

military
wasn't worried yet about school loans
my sister's asthma
the way my mama keeps trying
to cripple her want inside cake.

I used to carol at Christmas.
Part of some rookie chorus
our church started.
Their way of reaching out for the season
proclaiming the gold purse of God's love.
It didn't seem to matter much if our voices
couldn't keep up with us
as long as our hearts were willing.
We were told God forgives
will lighten our load.

Be loud! the youth minister would say
shout from the roof top Henry!
Remember children, God is listening.

I was learning to spell

the word *indenture*
it was for our history teacher
who liked talking about slavery
those old plantations in the South
that could make objects of grown
and not so grown people.

I wasn't sure I understood what he
was saying, was only eleven
knobby elbowed, smelling of the grease
my mama used to fleck in my hair.
My daddy claims each of us
has our own boots to fill
that being a man means learning to
sink or swim by your own juices
not blame the dark for deserting things.

My mama doesn't say much anymore
when he's talking to me
tells me *eat your oatmeal*
listen to the teachers as if somehow
they're going to save me.

She wears ice inside her bed slippers
burns the edge of my father's pancakes
then blankets them in thick syrup
so he won't notice
and we laugh under our breath

watch him gobble them up
like Christmas coming.

I don't like the way he talks to her
but I got nothing to do about it
keep my mouth shut
tell my baby sister to do the same
if she knows what's smart.

Already I have to keep her in line
watch those girls she plays with
make sure no one goes about
corrupting her mind
talking up makeup, the mall
their boyfriends
heathen gods that see over fence
get into panties
spike winter with fake lips.

The lights are glowing

always glowing
this time of year
like fountains
shiny dime store rings.

I am having trouble with Algebra Two
trouble with my brother
the teacher's pet peeves
way my family pretends
to be hemmed together
like paper cut people
with glued hands.

Tiny lights are sprinkled across
the houses as if Jesus is calling
some white, some flashing and rainbow
some dainty, others wide mannered
in their gaudy gaze.

I have not yet learned my way
around disaster
the perilous nature of landscapes
the way we can freeze so rock hard
not even the filler in our mittens
will save us.

Danny R's mother has been taken over
to the hospital in Burlington
no one knows what for

except that his daddy's working two jobs
and my mom keeps asking
what's going to happen to those kids?

These days we have a habit of eating more
mashed potatoes, baked beans.
My mama doesn't much like to cook anymore
but keeps doing it
not that my dad's words have a lot of
please in them.

Some Saturday nights
she is desperate for some laughs
drags him out for pizza
then to the Grange Hall up in Burksville.
Tells me he is never willing to dance
warns her that if she asks twice
she's likely to find her own way home
he'll walk out of there
no fooling.

There are lights dotting the houses
like tree tinsel.
It is the beginning of December.
School isn't yet let out.
My mama hasn't slipped on the ice yet
busted her leg.

The doctor hasn't sent the bills
there isn't yet the loss from her paycheck.

My daddy is splitting wood
probably imagining her young legs
bluesy promises
the way she used to bait him
when suddenly the fall is going to happen
her sobs spill across the side porch.

I watch him come from the wood shed
chuck his words out thin, hard as a nail board
why you damn as well done that girl!
as if he is scolding her
as if a woman can't afford thick ice on the steps
an accident
as if no man is going to be around
pick up the pieces
sooth a woman under the weight
of a busted leg.

It was the school play

my mama was coming.
She had a busted leg from the
unshoveled ice.
We'd scribbled all over the cast
with our yellow and blue names.

I was playing the Queen of Sheba
black eyeliner and a white sheet
gold braiding tacked to me
like wealth calling.

My mother said I had a clear voice
knew how to memorize
capture the audience with the
spell of my gaze.

It was the school play.
February when the sky is busted
a grey metal pot
won't speak nice to anybody.

I'd practiced for two months.
Ten lines and an encore.
Didn't come in late, annoy the teachers
with their chalk boards and cold coffee.

My brother never came.
He had gone into the military.
His first deployment.
Some *ticket to a future* he told me
the same one you'll someday need.

Not one of us talked about it
about war
the pricks and the plague.

Back then my mother's voice
hadn't collapsed on her
daddy hadn't yet taught me target practice
how to gut a gopher with his knife blade
slice out the bullshit.
He always had an eye for pretty girls
unsullied ones
liked to chat up my friends
didn't really see the actress in me
capable of hiding things
being the orator of blue shoes

capable of more than trailer parks
a plastic bird bath
county band stand
more than the leaking valve
of my mother's love.

It has been a bad day for forecasts

my daddy misread every one
a foot and a half of snow instead
of three inches
no detour in the mountains
Natie's pickup starting like a charm
when he gave it up as a block of ice
that would never thaw in her yard.

He is in a bad mood
taking it out on everybody.
Pitchforking our words so he
can stamp his face on them.
My mama can't do a right thing
not the eggs, the pancakes
the way her dress fits
not the color of the new curtain material
or the money she's been paid by Sally Gertz
for bringing the kids to school for two weeks
when their car broke down
and they were stuck five and a half miles
out of town with that busted wheel base.
Daddy says mama should never have agreed
to go to the store, do all that shopping
without bigger pay, extra thanks coming.

We don't say much at the table
just pour milk, eat pancakes
wonder about the holiday coming
whether grandpa's going to be up for it
and my mama going to make us come

get the tree at the tree farm
sing carols in the car
as if a shitload of new snow is falling.

I'm starting to be pissed at my sister's
slack words, the way she sashays
around our house like some showgirl
slops the plates on the table
spends hours hogging the bathroom
to straighten her hair.

Daddy claims she's the prettiest girl
he's seen this side of Atlanta
and my sister eats it up
spins for him like a party queen
gets him to buy her head scarves
a new pea jacket, sassy boots
while my mama looks on drab
as a baseboard.

I'm starting to get pissed off
at things but I ain't saying
pissed off over our meager stews
the way my mother indulges my sister
with her fantasies of acting school, dance team.

For years my daddy's been reminding me
how he works hard for every nickel and dime
busts his butt to put the meals on our table
that if he has some harsh words to say
when he comes in the door
maybe it's cause he feels dog tired, unappreciated

deserves somebody who pretties herself up
speaks with respect
not just canned hash, an overdone omelet

someone who understands
how a man takes a shitload
of responsibilities onto himself
free of charge
only asks in return for a little decency
a little sensible catering
a tasty meal, warm bed, soft voice
a woman who knows how to keep
her body, hours, good temperament
in line with God's love.

Over in Wattsville they're getting ready

for the Winter Pageant and Snow Festival.
Treena's in it.
Fourteen years old and slimmed down
as a birch tree.
My sister claims she's going to have to
put some extra padding in all the right places
if she's going to have a chance at the crown.

My sister has blue eyes so skyward
the high school boys kill for a glimpse of them.
I'm always needing to watch after
the length of her skirt
make sure God is leading.

She wants to be crowned Snow Queen
ride in the fake sleigh pulled by a black limo
wants the girls to think high of her
start inviting her to their skate parties
glam dances, gossip circle
as if she is miracle.

My mama half wants to be part of
the success story, sleepovers
hear the news
wants to preen Treena's hair
before a beggar world tames it.

My sister exiles the calories of cake
drudgery of chores
peril of my mama's face, its tractor driven folds

tucks her wants into a begging bowl
my father's racks of slain deer

folds her wants into the possibility
of Miss Snow Queen
the dazzle, lack of ice
celebrity brings.

I'm not going anywhere fast

I know that
though my daddy has plans for me
always has plans for me
so I won't be the disappointment
of my mom
who spot cleans his work pants
never manages to get out the stains.

He wants me to take up
pipefitting or else apprentice with
Stan Burton who runs the only
plumbing business in town
makes a decent wage
come autumn will be looking
for *one more good man.*

I don't see myself amounting to much.
Not yet.
Not with an accumulation of fence posts
my mama's polish trying to wipe over me.
My sister says she's going to state university
has big plans but I have no idea how she'll get there.
Doesn't even have the grades as far as I can see
but mama says *shut your sweet lips*
don't dare take the furnace out of her house walls
just *wait and see.*
Maybe my mama knows a pot of money I don't

or average grade reports that can be pencil erased
into honor roll if you know the right teacher.

My daddy calls me *lazy*.
Says when he was my age he was already
working after school delivering groceries
being a grease monkey on Saturdays
at his uncle's garage.
I tell him with the recession and all
it's the grownups taking the after school jobs
that I don't even have a driver's license
or a car to get places.

He shoots back
you're always making up excuses
trying to tell everyone how smart you are
thinking you better than the rest of us.
My mama will say *Lay off Dave*
but her words don't amount to anything.
What he says ain't true although sometimes
I find myself half believing him, half sure
I don't want to try anymore
sweep the fields
with so much snow falling.

This winter I broke my wrist
in a stupid accident playing skate ball.
My daddy says I'm a wimp
for needing painkillers afterwards

for a couple of days.
I'm still not sure my wrist healed right
if I can pitch the same ball.

My mama keeps pushing me to see
the doctor up in Meade, talks about
some sort of orthopedist there
but my pa won't hear none of it.
Says I just need a little exercise
that helping him out at the machine shop
would work out the kinks.

I'm not sure I'm going anywhere fast.
But I pretend.
Pretend I'm hard as a dump bell
hard as the jack knife in my daddy's pocket.
So hard my mama can barely
reach for me with her wispy ways
trays of English muffin pizza.
She makes me impatient
annoys the hell out of me
with the warm flap of her voice.

Part Five

Paradise on a Pole Stick

Am I a coward that counters the wind

keeps the world from looting
keeps my family intact
through a struggle of blue hands
half crinkled bed sheets?

I never believed god would desert me
turn a blind eye
refuse some cool breeze coming
to answer a heat wave.
Just that folks have lost
a ton of trust
think their own smart ass will
save them.

Someday I want to go straight into
the kitchen when my kids
my husband sitting at that table
and say – *I'm leaving here
packing up my life in the name
of her moonlight*
in the name of some more decent
kind of love.

Not sure even one of them would admit
to needing me.
They'll just get tunnel vision
marry their lives to new stuff

their phones, computer terminal
toys with anonymous strings.

God make me a station of your love
I keep praying
want to be the good handshake
decent neighbor, stop hearing
not quick enough
not useful enough
not clever enough
not sexy enough
as if those are the gauges and glitter
we marry

don't want to feel like some worn down thing
at the risk of perishing.

See you later

Everybody's saying that.
No time for anything.
Me foil wrapping the dinner
so it can be bird pecked later
in front of the t.v.

My girlfriend says they're
not worth the toil.
That most families break apart anyway
end the day with attorney fees
separate apartments, divided kids.

I don't want to hear such things.
She's talking out of her own mischief
the way her ex high tailed it out
of town without even a note
left her to raise three kids under seven
with a telephone service job, stack of bills.
Nobody's going to marry her quick
with the way her life is going.

See you later
as if we can carpet sweep things
into a metal incinerator
wake up in a new motel with a primped face
iced cokes, blue worship.

You tell me you *ain't going anywhere soon*
say that because I ask.
Ask you cause half the time

you barely seem to notice me
keep wondering if it's just my imagination.
Sometimes I ask the kids
but they say they don't want to get
in the middle of anything.

I ask *You want to be with me?*
If not, tell me straight up.
Course, darling.
You always say *Course, darling.*

For a day or two I go around
on cloud nine lifting
as if my shoes won't anchor.
Then the reality seeps in.
The way you scarcely notice me
care if I eat dinner
if I need help hauling in the groceries
what color dress I'm wearing
if I feel o.k. or sickly
about to die.

It's a creepy crawly inchworm

in the snow
nobody could have made it but you
the way you dark inked the white
out of her stretched skin
buttoned the face
as if she was marooned here
red eyed, forlorn.

January and your gloved hands
disguise things
the way your words, hands
build things up
snow shovel into mounds
you'll later crush.

The inchworm looks misplaced
stapled to one spot
netted with chicken wire
clots of snow that barely cover her ass.

You proclaim the artist in you
blush and squirm celebrity
watch while passersby take pics
dogs pee
children kick her side
as if it she is an emblem of something -
squat families, mangled toys.

It is like you to make a crucified
version of inchworm in the snow.

Peel back the skin
anchor a hard wedge.

Afterwards you want a beer, pub crawl
bragging rights, the flash of white teeth.
I watch the pearly gleam of you
the way you corrupt amber bottles
women, inchworms
insist on the agreeable
those of us willing to
hoist you up on a gold pulpit.

For how many hours, days, years

have I tried to please
smooth out creased shirts
offer up paradise on a pole stick
ignore the prickly
sidestep your blue pajamas
discharge the rain?

For how many summers
did I practice my Pentecostal
high wire act and green equators
try to set the house on fire
with the lace panties of my love?

How many times have I spot cleaned disaster
listened to a busted radio sing *you are the one*
watched you grow disdain
make all measuring sticks the sum
of other women's coo words?

For how long have I nursed a bruised father
the blank cover of his dust coat
watched him scalpel my play field
crew cut the lawn
force the roses into penitentiary?

Through how many storms of locust
haughty roads
did I wait for you, eat your thistle
believe that love rights any truancy
I could steer you safe into a room
holy with lamplight?

Part Six

The Language the Trees Preach

You won't believe it

I'm going soon
to some coastal town
miles of beach, a boardwalk
lack of February.

Millie R. is coming with me
arranging things
a week at some compact beach cottage
that overlooks the bay.
Haven't done something like this
in fifteen years.
She says I just need sunblock
a swimsuit, windbreaker
some flaming sleeveless dress
that rinses out the worn of me
won't fade.

Will I coax the sun into speechless
align my life with a rarer landscape
that few folks see
accept my pie eyed, dreamy
forgive your impatience
disdain
long held verdict that I am
not of this world

as if it's the ultimate flaw
tragic failure in me?

Was I made for love

Am I more than this soppy mess
puddled on the floor
more than pooled socks and pork roast
injured gingham?

Do each of us desire to find some true
persistent lover deep inside
who can witness
the glory and the sedge of us
the joys and the gypsy
welcome even our darkest night
not walk away

recognize that the earth
everything deep down
ambitions to hold us
tender as the snow.

My name is Dorothy

I have been a daughter to a fallen father
daughter to a young deceased mom
sister to a drug addict
mother to two children
wife of a man who hardly sees me
who ices my heart, offers up forked sex
marshals other women.
But still – I am more than this.

I said farewell yesterday
farewell to my old self
my crushed slippers
tied back hair
to stump toys with metal cannon
leashed yards
plastic wrapped meat
string bean lovemaking
said *goodbye* to his precious dishwasher
to tyrants who squash bugs, people
pistol words
turn the earth into thin summer
concrete what they think they own

said *goodbye* to the sinner's bible
sensible polyester
to school cafeteria jobs where we
serve canned peas and pop
am saying *yes* to my school girl longings
to frill skirts and fishnet

beach walks
a body that's naturally in love

I'm saying *yes* to long soaks
colored knee highs
extra slices of pumpernickel
to a negligee inside my street coat
saying *yes* to goofy love songs
saying *yes* to the earth's greening
tender words, decency
old people, the lost, unheard
yes to learning how to snowshoe
show my children how
glory wonderful
sacred the world can be.
I'm no longer holding back
letting the world's cynical eye
have its way

I'm saying *yes*
no permission requested
the birds squawking in my ear
flashing me with their obscene wings
the hum of the bees
making their thick globs of honey
out of my body's beehive.

It's the summer of my life coming

a virgin proposition
won't take *no* for an answer
says *yes* and *yes* and *yes*.
Two weeks ago my friend Julie
handed me the Aphrodite tarot card
said she was sure it was calling me.
On Saturday I decided to get
my hair tweaked
some auburn streaks, a few layers.

Starting to say *the hell* with nasty words
small minded manners
the way some people feel the need
to throw stone's in somebody else's
bathwater, pebble their voice.

I'm ready for potlucks and foraging
park benches
listening beside the river
a good dinner I don't have to earn
realize Henry's already gone into the military
Treena's out with her overzealous friends
flitting up a storm more than I wish
and that man of mine seems to be happy
if I spend my days eating rock hard candy
never socializing
filling my face with bowls of ice cream late night

while he hovers over his computer
with those private emails.

If the god of awe is a gentle being
tender
maybe it's time to stop pit bulling my life
settling for the less as though that's all
I deserve – a squat field paralyzed by want
while in my night field
rabbits are leaping
deer wander down from the woods
there are welcome kisses
no avalanched eye

my body pearl stitched
seasoned as the moon's
best housecoat.

Epilogue

Finch Feeding

Sometimes when we hear the memoir of a life

we want to hear birds flapping
the doze of unmuzzled grass.
In that story nobody shrivels up
dies of heart failure.
The man you love sees you into a sunset
fisted with blue bells, honeysuckle
streets team with children
long life dogs
a loyal voice calling.

That story is not the one I know
about a girl who doesn't get rolls royced through
the dirt stained streets, never jumps over punch
cards
food stamps, medical offices.
She grows up, learns to pack things
box dreams, children's lunch pails, marriage
wonder about the language the trees' preach.

In this story I am born in the middle of
a record July heat wave, every window
fan sold out at the store.
My mama reaches up to get a hat box
in those baby dolls that were made skimpy
enough to set men's eyes flaming, reaches up
when suddenly she can't make believe
any longer that I'm not coming
because I am coming and four hours later
drugged in the hospital delivery room

tied to a drip tray and white sheets
here I come into the world smelling of lilac.

I come out smelling of lilac so sure, incontestable
that for years afterwards my daddy grows lilacs
in the pint sized saga of our yard.
Come May clips a fist of them for my room
manages to curb his temper
around the scent of the blooms.

Did I tell you my mama was a dancer, a painter
the queen of cargo trunks and displaced shoes
that every fella she ever dated wanted to marry her
called her his *Liz Taylor look alike* and fiery red.
But after the Hollywood stuntman
after her return home it was my daddy
about to be stationed overseas
who she anchored with
hoped he would learn how to dance
make a green kingdom
Marlon Brando her life shimmery
as her platinum bracelets, slinky gowns.

My papa believed in the adage –
folks with big britches are in need of some manners training
and that's what he set about to do with me
after my mama was gone
and my brother was dealing with his elsewheres.
I crisscrossed rooms, spat at paper, did cartwheels

showed him my lazy eye
that never busts in a windstorm
wanted my papa to see the guile and roses of me.
He never did.

It helps for you to know my daddy's the product
of small town mills, distracted hands
boxed ears for not learning right how to tie shoes.
My dad's the product of a mother who died young
a messed up alcoholic dad, Catholic orphanage
too many schools.
I don't know if he feels abandoned by God
the way he does about people.
I wonder if he was always secretly afraid
my mama was going to be leaving him.

My daddy didn't know he was going to outlive
my mother and a second wife
someday need to come live with us.
But I'm getting ahead when I tell you all that.

This is just an opening verse, a small morsel of the
jagged saga, the memoir I'm going to find time
someday to write for you.
I want it to end up more than desolate
speak in the secret language of finch feeding

want you to know that, in the end
it's not a crime to stumble
eat up the snow
find a more compassionate God waiting.

Toni Thomas lives in Portland, Oregon. Her poems have been published in Austria, Spain, New Zealand, Canada, England, Scotland, and Australia. In the United States her work has appeared in over fifty literary magazines including *Prairie Schooner, North Dakota Quarterly, Hayden's Ferry Review, the Minnesota Review, Notre Dame Review, Poetry East*, and more. She has been twice nominated for a Pushcart prize, and won several awards. She has published twenty-two collections of poetry and six books for children.

Her figurative clay sculptures have been shown in gallery exhibits in Portland and Chicago, displayed in literary magazines, and housed in private collections in the U.S. and England.

Her short documentary *One of Us* was shown at the Trans-ideology: Nostalgia festival in Berlin and at the Museum of Contemporary Art in Taipei.

Since Toni loves to create and sits buried in reams of poems, manuscripts, clay figures and images….she likes to imagine all of them out in the world
swaying wild as the lupine.

tonithomaspoetry.com

www.ingramcontent.com/pod-product-compliance
Lightning Source LLC
Chambersburg PA
CBHW060620080526
44585CB00013B/914